Spelling Challenge

First Edition

by Marilyn More   Illustrated by Clifton Pugh

Introduction

How good are your students at spelling? Test your students spelling skills and improve their vocabulary with this Spelling Challenge workbook. Spelling Challenge will engage your students with challenging words that look similar in appearance, but only one is spelled correctly. Students must find the correctly spelled word and write the letter in the space provided in this multiple choice workbook. Answer sheets included at the end of this book.

How to use this book.

For each question provided, a number of similar words appear, but only one is spelled correctly and matches the clue that is provided. Students must write the letter of the correctly spelled word in the space by the question number.

Answer sheets located at the end of this workbook.

For each question below a number of similar words appear, but only one is spelled correctly and matches the clue that is provided. Write the letter of the correctly spelled word in the space by the question number.

1. ___ A. CHIEF B. CHEIF C. CFIEF D. CHIEFE
"He is the fire _____. He is in charge of all the firemen."

2. ___ A. INCLUD B. INCLUDE C. ENCLUDE D. INCCLUDE
Have as a part, to add to the whole.

3. ___ A. BECOMEE B. BECOME C. BCOM D. BECOM
"When I _____ president, I'm going to be famous."

4. ___ A. KONSUMER B. CONSUMIR C. CONSUMER D. CYNSUMER
A person who uses goods or services.

5. ___ A. SHID B. SLIDE C. SLAD D. SLID
Past tense of "slide."

6. ___ A. RELIGION B. RELIGIUN C. RELIGIONE D. RALIGION
A strong belief in a supernatural power or powers that control human destiny.

7. ___ A. WANDERRED B. WHANDERED C. WANDERED D. WANDIRED
Moved about without any destination.

8. ___ A. HOOKED B. HOKED C. HOOKEDE D. HOWKED
Curved downwards.

9. ___ A. HYDN'T B. HADNT C. HADN'T D. HADDN'T
Contraction for "had not."

10. ___ A. HY B. HIE C. RI D. HI
Used as a greeting.

For each question below a number of similar words appear, but only one is spelled correctly and matches the clue that is provided. Write the letter of the correctly spelled word in the space by the question number.

11. __   A. SUPPYSE   B. SUPPOCE   C. SUPOSE   D. SUPPOSE
     Synonym of "guess" and "imagine."

12. __   A. RATE   B. RAJE   C. REAT   D. RAT
     Amount of a charge or payment.

13. __   A. BEE   B. BE   C. BEE   D. BEE
     "Mike, why do you have to _____ so mean to your sister?"

14. __   A. SCAENTISTS   B. SSIANTISTS   C. STIANTISTS   D. SCIENTISTS
     Plural form of "scientist."

15. __   A. COMPETICIAN   B. COMPETITION   C. KOMPETITION   D. COMPETITIONE
     The act of competing as for profit or a prize; "There's going to be a big skateboarding _____ this weekend!"

16. __   A. COSTS   B. KOSTS   C. COSSS   D. COSTTS
     An expenditure, effort, or loss; "It _____ more to live in the city."

17. __   A. SERCH   B. CEARCH   C. SEARCH   D. SAIRCH
     Try to locate or discover, or try to establish the existence of.

18. __   A. CARYING   B. KARRYING   C. CARRYENG   D. CARRYING
     To be pregnant with; "I'm _____ his child."

19. __   A. RIYHT   B. RIT   C. REGHT   D. RIGHT
     Antonym of "left."

20. __   A. WOMAF   B. WOMANE   C. WOMAN   D. WAMAN
     An adult female person.

For each question below a number of similar words appear, but only one is spelled correctly and matches the clue that is provided. Write the letter of the correctly spelled word in the space by the question number.

21. __ A. SHOOT B. SHOOTE C. CHOOT D. SHOWT
To fire a shot.

22. __ A. WAT'S B. WHATS C. WHAT'S D. WHAT'D
Contraction of "what is."

23. __ A. BISTHDAY B. BIRTHDAE C. BIRTHDAY D. BIRTHDAYE
An anniversary of the day on which a person was born.

24. __ A. GARBIDGE B. GARBAGA C. GARBAG D. GARBAGE
She tossed the mouldy bread into the _____ can.

25. __ A. SHE B. SHEE C. SHEE D. SHEE
Female pronoun; a female, or something regarded as female, e.g. a ship.

26. __ A. ORDERD B. ERDERED C. ORDERED D. ORDERRED
Give instructions to or direct somebody to do something with authority.

27. __ A. O'CLLOCK B. OCLOCK C. O'CLOCK D. O'FLOCK
"Richard, be home at five _____ sharp!"

28. __ A. KNOT B. KNOT C. NOT D. KNOT
Negation of a word or group of words; "He does _____ speak French."

29. __ A. FOOL B. FUELL C. FUIL D. FUEL
Cars need _____ to run.

30. __ A. ALTHOUGH B. ALTHOGH C. ALTHOWGH D. ALVHOUGH
Despite the fact that.

For each question below a number of similar words appear, but only one is spelled correctly and matches the clue that is provided. Write the letter of the correctly spelled word in the space by the question number.

31. __ A. LEIST   B. LEASST   C. LEAST   D. LEASTE
Minimal in magnitude; the garter snake is the _____ dangerous snake.

32. __ A. DESKE   B. DESSK   C. DISK   D. DESK
A piece of furniture with a writing surface and usually drawers or other compartments.

33. __ A. STORES   B. STERES   C. STORRES   D. STTORES
Establishments for the retail sale of goods or services.

34. __ A. WICHES   B. WHISHES   C. WISHES   D. WISHESE
Plural form of "wish."

35. __ A. HOWEVER   B. HOUEVER   C. HOWEVR   D. HOWEVERE
Despite anything to the contrary.

36. __ A. ROGHTS   B. RITS   C. RIGTS   D. RIGHTS
Abstract ideas of that which are due by law, tradition, or nature.

37. __ A. WALKED   B. WALKD   C. WHALKED   D. WALKYD
Past tense of "walk."

38. __ A. SMEL   B. SMELLE   C. SMELL   D. SMELLL
Emit an odor.

39. __ A. WHOE   B. WHO   C. WHOE   D. WHOE
The one that.

40. __ A. MIROR   B. MERROR   C. MIRROR   D. MIRRER
Polished surface that forms images by reflecting light.

For each question below a number of similar words appear, but only one is spelled correctly and matches the clue that is provided. Write the letter of the correctly spelled word in the space by the question number.

41. ___ A. SIZE B. SIZEE C. SIZY D. SIZ
How big something is.

42. ___ A. ZIPPER B. ZIPPIR C. ZIPPUR D. ZIPPAR
A fastener for locking together two toothed edges by means of a sliding tab.

43. ___ A. MONSCERS B. MONSTERRS C. MONSTIRS D. MONSTERS
Plural form of "monster."

44. ___ A. GANG B. GANNG C. GANGE D. GUNG
An association of criminals.

45. ___ A. PAR B. PR C. PIR D. PER
For each, or for every.

46. ___ A. TEACHER B. TEACHR C. TECHER D. TEACHIR
A person whose profession is teaching.

47. ___ A. CRACK B. CRACKE C. CRYCK D. KRACK
A long narrow opening.

48. ___ A. DAUGHTAR B. DAGHTER C. DAUGGHTER D. DAUGHTER
One's female child.

49. ___ A. AUTOMOBIL B. AUTOMOBILLE C. AUTOMOBILE D. AUTOMOBELE
Synonym for car.

50. ___ A. SHALLL B. SHALLE C. SHALL D. SHAL
First person future; "I _____ do it."

For each question below a number of similar words appear, but only one is spelled correctly and matches the clue that is provided. Write the letter of the correctly spelled word in the space by the question number.

51. __ A. FATHERS B. FETHER'S C. FUTHER'S D. FATHER'S
"That is my _____ car."

52. __ A. ARRIVVED B. ARRIVED C. ARRIVD D. ARIVED
"The mail has not yet _____."

53. __ A. LIVONG B. LIVNG C. LIVING D. LIVIHG
True to life; lifelike.

54. __ A. BYZZ B. BUZ C. BUZZ D. BUZZE
The sound bees make.

55. __ A. CATLE B. CATTL C. CETTLE D. CATTLE
Domesticated bovine animals as a group regardless of sex or age.

56. __ A. MAKES B. MAKEF C. MAKESE D. MEKES
"Louise _____ a pretty good cake."

57. __ A. CHIPPING B. SHIPING C. SHIPPING D. SKIPPING
The commercial enterprise of transporting goods and materials.

58. __ A. GRASHOPPER B. GRASSHOPPAR C. GRASSHOPPIR D. GRASSHOPPER
An insect.

59. __ A. SEASON B. SEASONE C. CEASON D. SEISON
One of the natural periods into which the year is divided.

60. __ A. TUNNEL B. TUNEL C. TUNNELL D. TUNNEQ
A passageway through or under something.

For each question below a number of similar words appear, but only one is spelled correctly and matches the clue that is provided. Write the letter of the correctly spelled word in the space by the question number.

61. __ A. DRANNK B. DRINK C. DRONK D. DRANK
The past tense of "drink."

62. __ A. TO B. TO C. TO D. TOO
In addition.

63. __ A. MIDUTE B. MINUT C. MINUTTE D. MINUTE
A unit of time equal to 60 seconds or 1/60th of an hour.

64. __ A. NEXT B. NEXXT C. NOXT D. NEXTE
Antonym of "previous."

65. __ A. CONTYNT B. CONTENT C. KONTENT D. CONTUNT
Satisfy in a limited way; "He is very _____ with his artwork."

66. __ A. MEDIEM B. MEDDIUM C. MEDIUM D. MADIUM
Midway between extremes.

67. __ A. WAKE B. WHAKE C. WAKEE D. WAK
Stop sleeping.

68. __ A. DEGRES B. DEGREES C. DIGREES D. DEGREESE
"Is it ever hot out here! It must be at least forty _____ Celsius!"

69. __ A. KNOWLEDGE B. NOWLEDGE C. KNOWLEDGY D. KNOWLEGE
The result of learning.

70. __ A. INTWO B. INTWO C. INTO D. INTWO
Expresses a change of state; turn water _____ wine.

For each question below a number of similar words appear, but only one is spelled correctly and matches the clue that is provided. Write the letter of the correctly spelled word in the space by the question number.

71. ___ A. INJOYED   B. ENJOYER   C. ENJOYD   D. ENJOYED
Past tense of "enjoy."

72. ___ A. OPINION   B. OPINIUN   C. OPINAON   D. APINIAN
If it's not a fact, it is probably an _____.

73. ___ A. ROADSE   B. ROADS   C. ROIDS   D. ROADDS
Plural form of "road."

74. ___ A. BIKES   B. BAKES   C. BIKESE   D. BIKYS
There were two _____ locked in the bike stand.

75. ___ A. MINIBIKE   B. MINI-BIKE   C. MINI-BIK   D. MIQI-BIKE
A small motorcycle.

76. ___ A. SINNCE   B. SYNCE   C. SINC   D. SINCE
For the reason that; on account of; "_____ it's snowy, let's go skiing."

77. ___ A. SWI   B. SKA   C. SKIE   D. SKI
Narrow wood, metal, or plastic runners used for gliding over snow.

78. ___ A. HUSBAND   B. HUSSBAND   C. HUSBANDE   D. HUWBAND
A married man; a woman's partner in marriage.

79. ___ A. ANCE   B. ONSE   C. ONCE   D. ONCCE
As soon as; "_____ we are home, we can rest."

80. ___ A. YOUNGER   B. YOUNGR   C. YOUNPER   D. YOUNGIR
The antonym for "older."

For each question below a number of similar words appear, but only one is spelled correctly and matches the clue that is provided. Write the letter of the correctly spelled word in the space by the question number.

81. __ A. THESE B. THEIS C. THEIS D. THEIS
Plural of "this."

82. __ A. SONGS B. SUNGS C. SONGSE D. SOFGS
Plural form of "song."

83. __ A. SUPOSE B. SUPPOSEE C. SUPPOSE D. SEPPOSE
Synonym of "guess" and "imagine."

84. __ A. SPEAK B. SPEK C. SPEAKE D. SPEIK
To express in speech.

85. __ A. BESIDDES B. BESIDES C. BEHIDES D. BESEDES
Synonym of "likewise" and "as well".

86. __ A. THERD B. THIRRD C. THIRDE D. THIRD
One of three equal parts.

87. __ A. MARCH B. MARCHE C. MARCV D. MARCCH
This month falls right before April.

88. __ A. ADVERTISYNG B. ADVERTISENG C. ADVERTISING D. ADVERTISNG
A public promotion of some product or service.

89. __ A. ADAPTATON B. ADAPTATIUN C. ADAPTATIEN D. ADAPTATION
To get used to an environment.

90. __ A. LEGISLATION B. LEGISLATIEN C. LEGISLATON D. LEGGISLATION
The act of making or enacting laws.

For each question below a number of similar words appear, but only one is spelled correctly and matches the clue that is provided. Write the letter of the correctly spelled word in the space by the question number.

91. __ A. STTUFFED B. STUFED C. STUFFED D. STUFFD
Filled with something.

92. __ A. SETTLD B. CETTLED C. SETTLYD D. SETTLED
Established or decided beyond dispute or doubt.

93. __ A. ADULTSE B. ADULTTS C. ADULTS D. ADULZS
Fully developed people from maturity onward.

94. __ A. LETTINY B. LETING C. LETTING D. LETTINNG
"Is your mother _____ you go to the big concert next weekend?"

95. __ A. FENXE B. FENCO C. FENCE D. FANCE
A barrier that serves to enclose an area; "I want a nice house with a white picket _____."

96. __ A. TIGR B. TIGER C. TYGER D. TIGGER
Large feline of forests in most of Asia having a tawny coat with black stripes.

97. __ A. TANK B. TANKE C. TANNK D. TANW
An enclosed armored military vehicle; has a cannon and moves on caterpillar treads.

98. __ A. FEEL B. FEAL C. FEL D. FEEV
A property perceived by touch.

99. __ A. BIONEC B. BIONIC C. BIONICE D. BIONIK
"I'm going to take an advanced course in _____ engineering."

100. __ A. KONCERNED   B. CONCERND   C. CONCERNED   D. CONCIRNED
    Feeling or showing worry or solicitude.

ANSWER SHEETS

For each question below a number of similar words appear, but only one is spelled correctly and matches the clue that is provided. Write the letter of the correctly spelled word in the space by the question number.

1. A A. CHIEF   B. CHEIF   C. CFIEF   D. CHIEFE
   "He is the fire _____. He is in charge of all the firemen."

2. B A. INCLUD   B. INCLUDE   C. ENCLUDE   D. INCCLUDE
   Have as a part, to add to the whole.

3. B A. BECOMEE   B. BECOME   C. BCOM   D. BECOM
   "When I _____ president, I'm going to be famous."

4. C A. KONSUMER   B. CONSUMIR   C. CONSUMER   D. CYNSUMER
   A person who uses goods or services.

5. D A. SHID   B. SLIDE   C. SLAD   D. SLID
   Past tense of "slide."

6. A A. RELIGION   B. RELIGIUN   C. RELIGIONE   D. RALIGION
   A strong belief in a supernatural power or powers that control human destiny.

7. C A. WANDERRED   B. WHANDERED   C. WANDERED   D. WANDIRED
   Moved about without any destination.

8. A A. HOOKED   B. HOKED   C. HOOKEDE   D. HOWKED
   Curved downwards.

9. C A. HYDN'T   B. HADNT   C. HADN'T   D. HADDN'T
   Contraction for "had not."

10. D A. HY   B. HIE   C. RI   D. HI
    Used as a greeting.

For each question below a number of similar words appear, but only one is spelled correctly and matches the clue that is provided. Write the letter of the correctly spelled word in the space by the question number.

11. D A. SUPPYSE B. SUPPOCE C. SUPOSE D. SUPPOSE
Synonym of "guess" and "imagine."

12. A A. RATE B. RAJE C. REAT D. RAT
Amount of a charge or payment.

13. B A. BEE B. BE C. BEE D. BEE
"Mike, why do you have to _____ so mean to your sister?"

14. D A. SCAENTISTS B. SSIANTISTS C. STIANTISTS D. SCIENTISTS
Plural form of "scientist."

15. B A. COMPETICIAN B. COMPETITION C. KOMPETITION D. COMPETITIONE
The act of competing as for profit or a prize; "There's going to be a big skateboarding _____ this weekend!"

16. A A. COSTS B. KOSTS C. COSSS D. COSTTS
An expenditure, effort, or loss; "It _____ more to live in the city."

17. C A. SERCH B. CEARCH C. SEARCH D. SAIRCH
Try to locate or discover, or try to establish the existence of.

18. D A. CARYING B. KARRYING C. CARRYENG D. CARRYING
To be pregnant with; "I'm _____ his child."

19. D A. RIYHT B. RIT C. REGHT D. RIGHT
Antonym of "left."

20. C A. WOMAF B. WOMANE C. WOMAN D. WAMAN
An adult female person.

For each question below a number of similar words appear, but only one is spelled correctly and matches the clue that is provided. Write the letter of the correctly spelled word in the space by the question number.

21. A   A. SHOOT   B. SHOOTE   C. CHOOT   D. SHOWT
    To fire a shot.

22. C   A. WAT'S   B. WHATS   C. WHAT'S   D. WHAT'D
    Contraction of "what is."

23. C   A. BISTHDAY   B. BIRTHDAE   C. BIRTHDAY   D. BIRTHDAYE
    An anniversary of the day on which a person was born.

24. D   A. GARBIDGE   B. GARBAGA   C. GARBAG   D. GARBAGE
    She tossed the mouldy bread into the _____ can.

25. A   A. SHE   B. SHEE   C. SHEE   D. SHEE
    Female pronoun; a female, or something regarded as female, e.g. a ship.

26. C   A. ORDERD   B. ERDERED   C. ORDERED   D. ORDERRED
    Give instructions to or direct somebody to do something with authority.

27. C   A. O'CLLOCK   B. OCLOCK   C. O'CLOCK   D. O'FLOCK
    "Richard, be home at five _____ sharp!"

28. C   A. KNOT   B. KNOT   C. NOT   D. KNOT
    Negation of a word or group of words; "He does _____ speak French."

29. D   A. FOOL   B. FUELL   C. FUIL   D. FUEL
    Cars need _____ to run.

30. A   A. ALTHOUGH   B. ALTHOGH   C. ALTHOWGH   D. ALVHOUGH
    Despite the fact that.

For each question below a number of similar words appear, but only one is spelled correctly and matches the clue that is provided. Write the letter of the correctly spelled word in the space by the question number.

31. C A. LEIST B. LEASST C. LEAST D. LEASTE
Minimal in magnitude; the garter snake is the _____ dangerous snake.

32. D A. DESKE B. DESSK C. DISK D. DESK
A piece of furniture with a writing surface and usually drawers or other compartments.

33. A A. STORES B. STERES C. STORRES D. STTORES
Establishments for the retail sale of goods or services.

34. C A. WICHES B. WHISHES C. WISHES D. WISHESE
Plural form of "wish."

35. A A. HOWEVER B. HOUEVER C. HOWEVR D. HOWEVERE
Despite anything to the contrary.

36. D A. ROGHTS B. RITS C. RIGTS D. RIGHTS
Abstract ideas of that which are due by law, tradition, or nature.

37. A A. WALKED B. WALKD C. WHALKED D. WALKYD
Past tense of "walk."

38. C A. SMEL B. SMELLE C. SMELL D. SMELLL
Emit an odor.

39. B A. WHOE B. WHO C. WHOE D. WHOE
The one that.

40. C A. MIROR B. MERROR C. MIRROR D. MIRRER
Polished surface that forms images by reflecting light.

For each question below a number of similar words appear, but only one is spelled correctly and matches the clue that is provided. Write the letter of the correctly spelled word in the space by the question number.

41. A   A. SIZE B. SIZEE C. SIZY D. SIZ
How big something is.

42. A   A. ZIPPER B. ZIPPIR C. ZIPPUR D. ZIPPAR
A fastener for locking together two toothed edges by means of a sliding tab.

43. D   A. MONSCERS B. MONSTERRS C. MONSTIRS D. MONSTERS
Plural form of "monster."

44. A   A. GANG B. GANNG C. GANGE D. GUNG
An association of criminals.

45. D   A. PAR B. PR C. PIR D. PER
For each, or for every.

46. A   A. TEACHER B. TEACHR C. TECHER D. TEACHIR
A person whose profession is teaching.

47. A   A. CRACK B. CRACKE C. CRYCK D. KRACK
A long narrow opening.

48. D   A. DAUGHTAR B. DAGHTER C. DAUGGHTER D. DAUGHTER
One's female child.

49. C   A. AUTOMOBIL B. AUTOMOBILLE C. AUTOMOBILE D. AUTOMOBELE
Synonym for car.

50. C   A. SHALLL B. SHALLE C. SHALL D. SHAL
First person future; "I _____ do it."

For each question below a number of similar words appear, but only one is spelled correctly and matches the clue that is provided. Write the letter of the correctly spelled word in the space by the question number.

51. D A. FATHERS B. FETHER'S C. FUTHER'S D. FATHER'S
"That is my _____ car."

52. B A. ARRIVVED B. ARRIVED C. ARRIVD D. ARIVED
"The mail has not yet _____."

53. C A. LIVONG B. LIVNG C. LIVING D. LIVIHG
True to life; lifelike.

54. C A. BYZZ B. BUZ C. BUZZ D. BUZZE
The sound bees make.

55. D A. CATLE B. CATTL C. CETTLE D. CATTLE
Domesticated bovine animals as a group regardless of sex or age.

56. A A. MAKES B. MAKEF C. MAKESE D. MEKES
"Louise _____ a pretty good cake."

57. C A. CHIPPING B. SHIPING C. SHIPPING D. SKIPPING
The commercial enterprise of transporting goods and materials.

58. D A. GRASHOPPER B. GRASSHOPPAR C. GRASSHOPPIR D. GRASSHOPPER
An insect.

59. A A. SEASON B. SEASONE C. CEASON D. SEISON
One of the natural periods into which the year is divided.

60. A A. TUNNEL B. TUNEL C. TUNNELL D. TUNNEQ
A passageway through or under something.

For each question below a number of similar words appear, but only one is spelled correctly and matches the clue that is provided. Write the letter of the correctly spelled word in the space by the question number.

61. D A. DRANNK B. DRINK C. DRONK D. DRANK
The past tense of "drink."

62. D A. TO B. TO C. TO D. TOO
In addition.

63. D A. MIDUTE B. MINUT C. MINUTTE D. MINUTE
A unit of time equal to 60 seconds or 1/60th of an hour.

64. A A. NEXT B. NEXXT C. NOXT D. NEXTE
Antonym of "previous."

65. B A. CONTYNT B. CONTENT C. KONTENT D. CONTUNT
Satisfy in a limited way; "He is very _____ with his artwork."

66. C A. MEDIEM B. MEDDIUM C. MEDIUM D. MADIUM
Midway between extremes.

67. A A. WAKE B. WHAKE C. WAKEE D. WAK
Stop sleeping.

68. B A. DEGRES B. DEGREES C. DIGREES D. DEGREESE
"Is it ever hot out here! It must be at least forty _____ Celsius!"

69. A A. KNOWLEDGE B. NOWLEDGE C. KNOWLEDGY D. KNOWLEGE
The result of learning.

70. C A. INTWO B. INTWO C. INTO D. INTWO
Expresses a change of state; turn water _____ wine.

For each question below a number of similar words appear, but only one is spelled correctly and matches the clue that is provided. Write the letter of the correctly spelled word in the space by the question number.

71. D A. INJOYED B. ENJOYER C. ENJOYD D. ENJOYED
Past tense of "enjoy."

72. A A. OPINION B. OPINIUN C. OPINAON D. APINIAN
If it's not a fact, it is probably an _____.

73. B A. ROADSE B. ROADS C. ROIDS D. ROADDS
Plural form of "road."

74. A A. BIKES B. BAKES C. BIKESE D. BIKYS
There were two ____ locked in the bike stand.

75. B A. MINIBIKE B. MINI-BIKE C. MINI-BIK D. MIQI-BIKE
A small motorcycle.

76. D A. SINNCE B. SYNCE C. SINC D. SINCE
For the reason that; on account of; "_____ it's snowy, let's go skiing."

77. D A. SWI B. SKA C. SKIE D. SKI
Narrow wood, metal, or plastic runners used for gliding over snow.

78. A A. HUSBAND B. HUSSBAND C. HUSBANDE D. HUWBAND
A married man; a woman's partner in marriage.

79. C A. ANCE B. ONSE C. ONCE D. ONCCE
As soon as; "_____ we are home, we can rest."

80. A A. YOUNGER B. YOUNGR C. YOUNPER D. YOUNGIR
The antonym for "older."

For each question below a number of similar words appear, but only one is spelled correctly and matches the clue that is provided. Write the letter of the correctly spelled word in the space by the question number.

81. A   A. THESE   B. THEIS   C. THEIS   D. THEIS
Plural of "this."

82. A   A. SONGS   B. SUNGS   C. SONGSE   D. SOFGS
Plural form of "song."

83. C   A. SUPOSE   B. SUPPOSEE   C. SUPPOSE   D. SEPPOSE
Synonym of "guess" and "imagine."

84. A   A. SPEAK   B. SPEK   C. SPEAKE   D. SPEIK
To express in speech.

85. B   A. BESIDDES   B. BESIDES   C. BEHIDES   D. BESEDES
Synonym of "likewise" and "as well".

86. D   A. THERD   B. THIRRD   C. THIRDE   D. THIRD
One of three equal parts.

87. A   A. MARCH   B. MARCHE   C. MARCV   D. MARCCH
This month falls right before April.

88. C   A. ADVERTISYNG   B. ADVERTISENG   C. ADVERTISING   D. ADVERTISNG
A public promotion of some product or service.

89. D   A. ADAPTATON   B. ADAPTATIUN   C. ADAPTATIEN   D. ADAPTATION
To get used to an environment.

90. A   A. LEGISLATION   B. LEGISLATIEN   C. LEGISLATON   D. LEGGISLATION
The act of making or enacting laws.

For each question below a number of similar words appear, but only one is spelled correctly and matches the clue that is provided. Write the letter of the correctly spelled word in the space by the question number.

91. C   A. STTUFFED B. STUFED C. STUFFED D. STUFFD
    Filled with something.

92. D   A. SETTLD B. CETTLED C. SETTLYD D. SETTLED
    Established or decided beyond dispute or doubt.

93. C   A. ADULTSE B. ADULTTS C. ADULTS D. ADULZS
    Fully developed people from maturity onward.

94. C   A. LETTINY B. LETING C. LETTING D. LETTINNG
    "Is your mother _____ you go to the big concert next weekend?"

95. C   A. FENXE B. FENCO C. FENCE D. FANCE
    A barrier that serves to enclose an area; "I want a nice house with a white picket _____."

96. B   A. TIGR B. TIGER C. TYGER D. TIGGER
    Large feline of forests in most of Asia having a tawny coat with black stripes.

97. A   A. TANK B. TANKE C. TANNK D. TANW
    An enclosed armored military vehicle; has a cannon and moves on caterpillar treads.

98. A   A. FEEL B. FEAL C. FEL D. FEEV
    A property perceived by touch.

99. B   A. BIONEC B. BIONIC C. BIONICE D. BIONIK
    "I'm going to take an advanced course in _____ engineering."

100. <u>C</u> A. KONCERNED B. CONCERND C. CONCERNED D. CONCIRNED
Feeling or showing worry or solicitude.

31437021R00020

Made in the USA
Lexington, KY
20 February 2019